SILVER BOOK BOX

HOW A FILM IS MADE

Silver Book Box
Series Editor: Julia Eccleshare

Why the Agouti Has No Tail Floella Benjamin
The Computer Nut Betsy Byars
Not Many People Know That! Michael Caine
Real Life Monsters Richard Davis
Grow Your Own Poems Peter Dixon
Is That It? Bob Geldof
How a Film is Made Bruce Purchase
Journey of 1000 Miles Ian Strachan

SILVER BOOK BOX

HOW A FILM IS MADE

Bruce Purchase

MACMILLAN EDUCATION

For Elspeth, Josie and Reuben

©Bruce Purchase 1988

All rights reserved. No reproduction, copy or transmission of this publication may be made without written permission.

No paragraph of this publication may be reproduced, copied or transmitted save with written permission or in accordance with the provisions of the Copyright Act 1956 (as amended), or under the terms of any licence permitting limited copying issued by the Copyright Licensing Agency, 33-4 Alfred Place, London WC1E 7DP.

Any person who does any unauthorised act in relation to this publication may be liable to criminal prosecution and civil claims for damages.

First published 1988

Published by
MACMILLAN EDUCATION LTD
Houndmills, Basingstoke, Hampshire RG21 2XS
and London
Companies and representatives
throughout the world

Designed by Julian Holland

Cover: photograph by the author;
  design by Julian Holland

Printed in Hong Kong

British Library Cataloguing in Publication Data
Purchase, Bruce
How a film is made. — (Silver book box).
1. Lionheart (Motion picture)
I. Title II. Series
791.43'0232   PN1997.L/
ISBN 0-333-44686-0

CONTENTS

A note on the author 6

Waiting for the phone to ring 9
The script 10
Costumes 13
Make-up 15
Lionheart 18
Budapest 20
The horses 22
Battle scenes 25
Stunts 28
And blood... 29
Waiting in the cold 31
The caterers 34
The actor's day 36
Rehearsals and takes 38
Processing the film 41
Cameras and sound 42
Special effects 46
Lighting 46
Building sets, making props 48
The children 51
The plot 54
Portugal, a new location 57
The end? 59
Editing, post-synching 60
Publicity 61
Finis 62

The unit list 64
Glossary 66
Book list 72

A note on the author
Bruce Purchase was born in New Zealand and came to the UK on a New Zealand government bursary to study acting at RADA.

He was a founder acting member of the National Theatre, under the direction of Laurence Olivier, and has also been for several years a member of the Royal Shakespeare Company, Nottingham Playhouse and the Bristol Old Vic. He played the title role of Othello to Bernard Miles' Iago at the Mermaid Theatre.

His film credits include *Mary, Queen of Scots* and *Macbeth*; and he has worked for many years in television, including such series as *I, Claudius*, *Dr Who*, *Clayhanger*, and as Squire Trelawney in *Return to Treasure Island*.

The film *Lionheart* was made in Hungary and Portugal during the months of November 1985 to March 1986. The executive producers were Francis Ford Coppola and Jack Schwartzman, and the company which made the film was Taliafilm II (UK) Ltd, with Talia Shire producing and Franklin Schaffner as director. *Lionheart* was first released in 1987.

The photographs in this book are all the author's own, and thus convey a true 'actor's eye-view' of filming. The italic words in the text can be found in the glossary.

Acknowledgements
I would like to thank Brenda Stones whose advice on the structure and sequence of this book was invaluable. Also thanks to my friends on *Lionheart* who shared the experience.

Thanks are due to Talia Shire and to Taliafilm II UK Ltd for the reproduction of a page of the script of *Lionheart*.

A typical moment showing all the people involved on a film-set.

Key to photograph
1 First Assistant Director
2 Focus-puller
3 Camera Operator
4 Clapper/Loader
5 Dresser (Hungarian)
6 Continuity Clerk
7 Dresser (Hungarian)
8 Boom Operator
9 Sound Recordist
10 Make-up
11 Hungarian Assistant Director
12 Boy actor
13 Director's daughter
14 Interpreter
15 Stuntman
16 Extras
17 Costume Designer's assistant

Waiting for the phone to ring

How does an actor spend the greatest part of his life? Waiting, endlessly waiting!

Some people call it 'resting', but that's hardly a fair description of how I spend my time between jobs: there I was, at the top of a stepladder, paint-pot in hand, filling in time with some home decorating. Trying to take my mind off the telephone and whether it was ever going to ring...

Suddenly, as I had the brush stuck stickily in the pot, the phone did ring. Help! Trying not to drip white emulsion over everything, including the dog, I leapt down the ladder and grabbed the phone with my paint-bespattered hand.

Well, said my agent, how would I like to spend six weeks in Hungary and three in Portugal, playing in a film about the Children's Crusade? Would I like it! You bet, I said, remembering in time to ask what the part was like and what the fee might be if I got the job.

My agent, Joyce, is my best support in my working life: she suggests my name to casting directors as available for suitable parts, arranges meetings with film directors (or TV and stage directors), then haggles for fees and schedules that will give me the best possible deal.

My agent had fixed the meeting with the film's *director*, Franklin Schaffner, a veteran of Hollywood, who made *Nicholas and Alexandra*, *Papillon*, and *Planet of the Apes* and dozens of

The author, 'resting'

other films. I was given a brief interview at Pinewood Studios, home of *Star Wars* and all the James Bond films. We talked about how he conceived the new film and about the part he was considering me for. We had met once years before but had never worked together. He did not ask me to read a scene from the script, as sometimes does happen, and after fifteen minutes our meeting ended. I left not knowing whether I'd get the part.

Then here was Joyce saying yes, the offer had come through and the whole deal had been agreed. Later that day, the script was on its way to me by motorbike messenger.

The script

Reading a new script for the first time is an exciting moment. I tend to read the whole thing through to myself, many times, letting my imagination run but not deciding yet how I will actually play the part.

The script at this stage is not necessarily the final *shooting script*, and it has progressed through many versions since it was originally commissioned. In the run-up to the start of filming, replacement re-write pages sometimes arrive through the letterbox, denoting each stage of re-writing the script. The production office will often ring to say, 'Have you received the blue pages...yellow pages...pink pages, etc.?' In fact, with this film, the script changed very little from the version that was first delivered to me, indicating general agreement on the scriptwriter's work.

A page from the film-script

```
1   INT. COUNT NERRA'S CASTLE - GREAT HALL - (CONTINUED)   1

                    NERRA
           ... You propose to pay for your
           sins by joining a foreign lord in
           a foreign land in a battle that
           isn't your own?

                    DE MONTFORT
           Why fight your countrymen when
           a common enemy exists in the
           Holy Land?...

                    NERRA
           First a knight must be faithful
           to his Lord.

   Robert listens intently to the exchange.

                    DE MONTFORT
           Hasn't the House of Nerra
           gathered enough land?

                    NERRA
           The House of Nerra will have
           gathered enough land when the
           whole of France lies at its
           feet!

                    DE MONTFORT
           I ask your blessing, Simon.

                    NERRA
           I won't have it, Charles.

   Robert steps forward impulsively.

                    ROBERT
           Father...

   All eyes turn to Robert, who's glancing back and forth
   from De Montfort to Nerra, torn by his respect for both
   men.

   Nerra throws a commanding stare at De Montfort.

   De Montfort, recognizing the boy's confusion, respects
   Nerra's wishes.

                                        (CONTINUED)
```

Reading through, and imagining the role

Once we all get together on the *set* the script develops as the chemistry of these particular actors starts to work and the words on the page begin to come alive.

But for the time being, preparation just meant getting totally familiar with the character I was going to play, and imagining how I might look and behave.

Our director Franklin Schaffner, seen on location in Portugal

Costumes

In the fortnight before I left for Hungary, I was measured for all the costumes I would need. These included metal helmets, leather trousers, fur jerkins, and armour. Armour is usually made of glass fibre so that it will not be too heavy to wear in horse-riding and fighting scenes. Just imagine what it was like for the actual medieval knights going into battle with all the weight of real chain-mail and armour!

Dressed up to kill!

Costumes for films are usually hired, or made by specialist firms who have access to special resources and ready-made costumes for whichever period is required. They have floor-upon-floor of wonderful costumes to choose from. The biggest and best of these costumiers are based in London, and serve the film industry worldwide.

However, for this film, all the costumes were to be made in Rome and on *location* in both Hungary and Portugal, under the direction of a gifted Italian designer called Nana Cecchi. My measurements had to be phoned through so that her drawings for at least the first costume could be transformed into reality within fourteen days.

In addition to the costumes for the twenty-five *principal actors*, many hundreds of other

The costume of King Richard himself, with the first assistant director in the background

costumes were already made for all the crowd *extras* and for the dozens of riders involved in the battles.

Nana and her team had actually been working on the creation of these costumes for months before filming began, and she herself had spent six months before that, making detailed drawings of each individual costume.

Costume-making is a gigantic operation giving work to many assistants, who transform the designer's drawings into actual costumes. In the case of this film Nana even had special cloth handwoven by craftspeople in northern Italy.

Make-up

Another important meeting before I left was with Pat, the Head of Make-up, and with Meinir, Chief Hair Stylist. This took place in London. They told me that the director wanted the entire Nerra family, of whom I was the father, to be red-headed. With time so short they asked if I would mind having my hair dyed, rather than wearing a wig which would have to be specially made. My preference anyway was for dyeing the hair, as I disliked wearing wigs. In fact I kept the same colour for the film I did after this one. So my friends got used to me being a red-head!

The next demand was for a long scar down my cheek, so that I would look the true battle-scarred warrior. It is amazing how scars are made: Pat, of make-up, tried creating a plaster cast of my head, which meant covering my face with wet plaster while I breathed through straws stuck up my nose! I had had it done once previously for *Dr Who*, so I knew what I was in for.

The casing took fifteen minutes to dry. When it had hardened it was removed and filled in at the back to make a complete mask of my face. Pat hoped to use this frame to shape scars from rubber latex, which would then be glued to my face. As so often happens, after all the time on this experiment, Pat then decided another method might be simpler, and even more effective.

The scar in place

Pat, of make-up, on set

So now they tried painting the scars straight on to my face. First the vivid colour of the scar was painted on to the skin and then a colourless liquid plastic was painted on, one coat after another, and left to dry. This caused the skin to tighten. We ended up with a gruesome and very realistic scar indeed.

At this first meeting with Pat and Meinir I was shown Nana's drawings of what my character in costume was meant to look like. With the full appearance of clothing, hair and facial make-up now in mind, I began to create a more living picture of how Simon Nerra would behave.

My 'son' Robert, played by Eric Stolz, leading the children out of Paris

Lionheart

You must be wondering by now who on earth I was going to play. My character, Simon Nerra, was all of this: a French duke, in an American film, set in twelfth-century France, but filmed in Hungary and later in Portugal. The reason for this complication of location was purely cost: it is cheaper to represent northern France in Hungary and southern France in Portugal. Films cost millions of dollars to make, so it is necessary for the *producer* to squeeze every possible saving. It is actually quite common for film teams these days to be miniature United Nations, picking up local talent in whichever country they are located.

The crusade departs

The film was called *Lionheart, the Children's Crusade*, and was woven round the true story of a band of children who left Paris in the twelfth century to join the English King, Richard the Lionheart, intending to travel with him to the Holy Land. The film gave parts to hundreds of children and *extras* who would play crusaders, and the hope was that it would appeal to a very wide, international audience.

Budapest

At last, after all this preparation, I was ready for off. The day I left my home in Oxford I was picked up by a chauffeur-driven car for the drive to Heathrow Airport. Light snow was falling as we took off, but when we landed in Budapest the snow lay thick on the ground. Budapest is the capital of Hungary and has been described as 'the Paris of the East'. It is an overwhelmingly beautiful city. From the first moment I arrived there it struck me as very foreign and quite magical, and I remained captivated throughout my stay.

I had just settled into my hotel room when the phone began to ring (that phone again!). Arrangements had to be made to meet Pat and Meinir, in the make-up room in the hotel; then Nana, in the costume department, to try on my first costume. Next came a summons to the *studio* to show Franklin, the director, what my whole appearance looked like. He greeted me in the studio, with the enigmatic phrase: 'Welcome to the twelfth century!'

I was then invited to meet others on the *unit*, like the *first assistant director*, the *second assistant director*...all this arranged by the *third assistant director*, who was in fact the constant voice on the phone.

Later I met a friend, also working on the film, and after we had collected our daily expense money paid in the local currency, we went on for dinner in a small nearby restaurant. A violinist and singer serenaded us at table, and

I remember that when they discovered we were English they played the Beatles' song 'Yesterday', following it up with 'John Brown's Body' and 'Daisy, Daisy'! What a long first day. I was tired that night, and fell asleep easily.

Budapest at dawn

The horses

On the second day I started horse-riding. I had ridden ever since my early childhood in New Zealand, but I needed practice again now. It was a question of both exercising my muscles and getting familiar with my horse before work began, in full armour and costume.

Dozens of horses were needed for the battle scenes in the film, so the stables were full. It was a nice job for the grooms, I thought, training and exercising on the film set.

The horses were very beautiful Hungarian creatures, and mine was a tall chestnut mare called Pritzi. I became very fond of her. She had

The horses, in wintry landscape

a baby foal which was always taken to *location*, so that she would not miss her mother.

Another of the horses we all specially remember was a gorgeous little pony ridden by one of the children; this pony became a great favourite with all the cast. But she was terribly difficult to balance on at a trot (rather roly-poly), and the young actress who rode her was often thrown. Luckily the girl was never injured because it was not that far to the ground!

Those horses that had been *established*, or made familiar on film, were taken on to Portugal, for the final part of filming. This included my 'son' Robert's beautiful big white horse. Most of the grooms in Hungary were from a circus but the grooms in Portugal were soldiers in the Portuguese army.

Positioning the horses

A dramatic shot: cameramen up on a crane against the Budapest skyline

The other animal-part in the film which I particularly remember was the falcon: she was a beautiful creature, and the falconer who had to attend her all the time and guide her flying gave me a chance to feed her with tiny pieces of red meat. The falcon is a real 'star' in the film and was breathtaking in flight. For the last *shot* in the film the falcon was chosen as the focus, soaring upwards towards camera.

Battle scenes

Lionheart required two big battle scenes in the course of the story, and other smaller skirmishes.

The process of filming a battle takes an incredible amount of time. This is because each little scene has to be prepared, rehearsed and acted out, with all the movement precisely controlled. When all these dozens of short 'moments' are finally put together in the *editing room* they are seen as continuous action, whereas every little 'blow' or 'kill' has to be carefully set up, lit, rehearsed and filmed individually.

One of the battle scenes took a week to make. Can you guess how long it will be in the finished film? About four minutes! A very slow process in order to get the action absolutely right. The actual 'pace' of the whole scene would be created much later in the *cutting room*. But more about that later.

With the many horses and riders in different costumes, depicting the opposing armies, tremendous organisation was necessary before the camera started *rolling*, the sound started *running* and '*Action*' was called.

The horses had to be handled gently, as they can so easily become frightened, making it difficult to get them to obey the action planned for a particular scene.

Wearing the armour was far from comfortable, and the combination of swinging a sword with the necessary force to be thought believable, while controlling a nervous horse, was never easy. But the object is to make it all look natural in the finished film, so that the audience in the cinema feel as if they are watching real people performing real actions, rather than just actors pretending.

27

Stunts

For the battle scenes, the key person is the stunt-coordinator. Ours was called Peter, and his job was to hire trained stuntmen and one stuntwoman, for the most dangerous parts of the action. Peter was in overall charge of handling the stunts, which he planned out in great detail, at all costs avoiding the likelihood of accidents. Whenever an actor had to be shot by an arrow, or fall from a galloping horse, this was done by the stuntperson dressed up in the actor's costume. These moments are so brief that you, as a member of the general viewing public, would find it difficult to see the difference

Preparing for battle stunts, and painting on the blood

between the actual actor and the stunt-double. Mind you, on video, you can press the pause button and *freeze frame*. Try it. See if you can spot the difference.

If an actor were to be injured doing a stunt, valuable time and money would be lost, so the stuntperson 'pretends' to be the actor. A risk was taken in one film I did many years ago when an actor did a stunt himself. He ended up with a sword-slashed face, requiring plastic surgery. Hence the need for a trained substitute.

In fact actors are forbidden in their contract from doing any dangerous activities during the making of a film, including flying in private aircraft, skiing, skating or any other such sports. If an actor is injured, too much money would be lost through hold-ups in *shooting*.

In Hungary our stuntmen came from a circus, and performed miracles of difficult horsemanship. They would fall from their mounts at great speed without injury and even made horses fall to the ground at a full gallop, without damage to mount or rider.

And blood...

The blood you see in a film is of course imitation. It comes in different thicknesses depending on whether it is required to be matted, half congealed or flowing freely. Make-up artists easily improvise their own blood from anything they can find in the kitchen cupboard, including colouring like cochineal!

I was once in a film when so much 'blood' was used in one day that the supply was completely used up. The director was furious and called for more, but neither *props* nor make-up had a drop left. Finally they had to improvise with the help of a huge can of raspberry jam (pips and all!) commandeered from the caterers in the studio kitchen. The 'dead' body of a huge brown bear was smeared with it and it actually looked very realistic.

All kinds of tricks can be used to get the right effect of bleeding. For instance, if a character is meant to be 'stabbed', you can place a pouch of 'blood' next to his skin, behind the costume. Then when the 'killing' blow is delivered, a nozzle can be squeezed and the 'blood' is seen to seep realistically through the costume.

Also 'blood capsules' can be kept in the mouth and bitten just at the right time so that the 'blood' dribbles from the corner of the mouth! It does not actually taste of anything much!

One warrior in his dying throes

Waiting in the cold

With only brief breaks in the weather it remained intensely cold in Hungary, and we could only look forward to warmer times in Portugal. Snow often lay deep on the ground, and fire hoses had to be used to clear the snow in the area where we were filming. Temperatures were more often than not well below freezing. We had to wear thick thermal underwear under our costumes. The poor children suffered most because of all the hanging about in Arctic temperatures, but there were lots of blankets to wrap up in while they waited.

In between *takes*, or during scenes that did not involve us, we would retreat to the caravans where we were lodged on *location*. Although cramped, they were comfortable and warm.

A combination of cold and fatigue!

My 'son' outside his caravan

There we would read, play Scrabble and chess and listen to music. On those rare days when the weather was milder, we would sit outside our caravans, enjoying for the moment a touch of sun.

The most boring times were when the big crowd scenes were being *staged* outside and we just had to be there on the *set*, either rehearsing or waiting for all the technical problems to be sorted out: lights being set up, cameras being placed, horses manoeuvred, carts dragged out of mud, crowd *extras* being placed in position or told where to move, etc.

Then there was no escape from numb fingers.

My own caravan, in a rare moment of sun

Wrapped up between two make-up girls!

33

The caterers

The caterers are crucial: you need gallons of continuous coffee and heaps of hot food to keep everyone happy and warm. The caterers came from Spain. I had worked with them before, in Czechoslovakia, so it was good to meet up with them and eat their delicious food again. They are among the best professional film unit caterers in Europe. Rafael and his team have huge mobile kitchens and can provide excellent food for several hundred people at a time.

Sometimes we would have lunch together in large heated tents, but more often than not my *dresser*, Agnes, would get some food for me and

See the signpost pointing towards the location-site

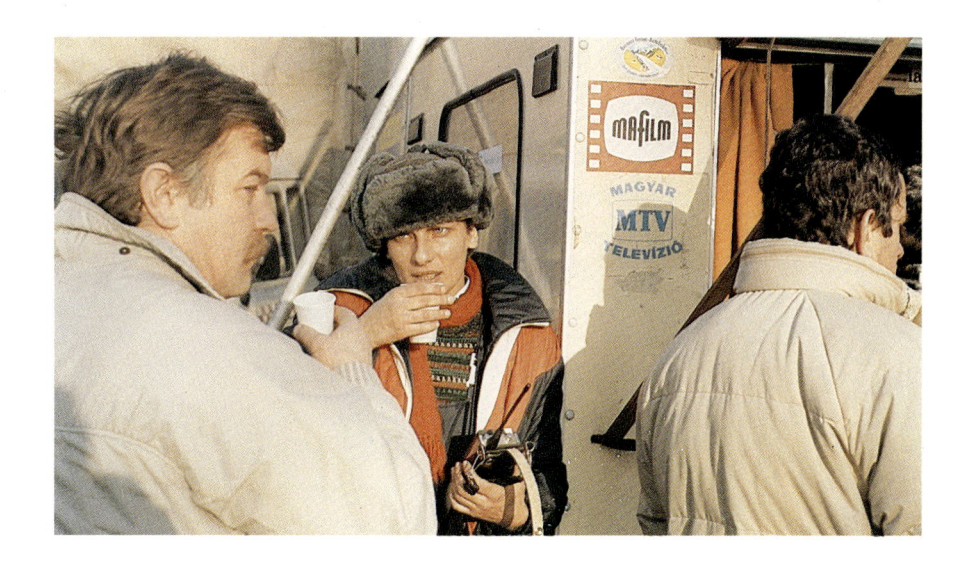

bring it to my caravan, thus avoiding the need to line up for food, especially when it was snowing.

The demands on the caterers never ended through day and night: we would arrive at seven in the morning, expecting breakfast of bacon rolls, butties, scrambled eggs, etc. before our first scene of the day.

Then at lunch-time a three-course meal was provided with several choices to please everyone, and in the mid-afternoon a selection of freshly baked cakes and sandwiches was set out, to keep us happy!

If it was a *night shoot* there was a *running buffet* throughout the night. At four in the morning a brief snack is desperately needed to keep you awake and improve concentration.

You can see how difficult it is for the caterers at the best of times, but just imagine when they are called on to cater for three hundred people at the top of a mountain with two feet of snow on the ground!

The Hungarian dressers having coffee at their mobile canteen

My dresser Agnes, enjoying breakfast with one of the Hungarian wardrobe staff

The actor's day

The routine of film-making means a long working day and a long working week. It was always a six-day week with only Sundays free. Every morning we were up at five and whisked off by car to the location or the studio. The locations were often an hour's drive away, so our bases there were the caravans.

The day's work would go on until about four on location, when the light began to fail; but in the studio we would carry on often until eight at night. Then the first assistant would call out 'It's a *wrap*', signalling end of filming for the day. At that call several hundred technicians, actors and

45th DAY OF SHOOTING		CALL SHEET			DATE December 4th, 1986	
SHOOTING CALL				NO.		
PICT. CASANOVA					DIR. Simon Langton	
SET INT. FORT ST. ANDREA			SCS. 8-8A 7-9	1/8	LOC. Estudios Roma	
SET INT. CELL. DAY			SCS. 9	1 2/8	LOC. " "	
SET INT. CELL CASANOVA - NIGHT			SCS. 9A	2/8	LOC. " "	
SET INT. FORT ST. ANDREA - DAY			SCS. 52	1/8	LOC. " "	
SET INT. CELL ST. ANDREA. DAY			SCS. 53	1/8	LOC. " "	
SET INT. CASANOVA'S CELL - DAY			SCS. 55	3/8	LOC. " "	
SET INT. NEW CELL LEADS			SCS. 80A	3/8	LOC. " "	
SET INT. LEADS ATTIC - DAY			SCS. 75	4/8	LOC. " "	
SET INT. LEADS ATTIC			SCS. 75A,B,C	2/8	LOC. " "	
SET EXT. LEADS ROOF. NIGHT			SCS. 81	3/8	LOC. " "	
CAST AND DAY PLAYERS		PART OF	MAKEUP	SET CALL	REMARKS	
Richard Chamberlain		Casanova	6'45am	8'30am	Leave 6'30am	
Bruce Purchase 7-12		Grandi	8'45am	9'30am	Leave 7:00am 8-30	
Roy Kinnear		Balbi	9-15am 12-15	1'00	Leave 10:00am 12-00	
Brian Handley		Surgeon	9-15am 12-15	9-30am 1'00	Leave 8:00am 12-00	
M. Balfour		Jailer	7'15	8-30	" 7-00	

ATMOSPHERE AND STANDINS		THRU GATE	
2 Prisoners		7'00am	
1 Officier		7'00am	
2 Turnkeys		7'00am	
2 Guards		7'00am	

ADVANCE FRIDAY: Sc. 83. Int. Place. Night. 1/8
 Sc. 82. Ext. Leads roof. Night. 1,2/8
 Sc. 68. Int. Casanova's cell. Day. 2/8
 Sc. 68A. Int. Casanova's cell. 1/8
 Sc. 57. Int. Casanova's cell. Night. 1/8
 Sc. 60. Int. Casanova's cell. Night. 2/8

ASST. DIR. JOE OCHOA/ IÑIGO VALLEJO-NAGERA   UNIT PROD. MGR. JOSE MARIA RODRIGUEZ

everyone else made a dash for whatever transport was available, back to the hotel, hot bath and a light meal.

A call sheet from the film *Casanova*

At about nine in the evening the next day's *call sheet* was slipped under the door. This tells you which scenes will be worked on the following day so that you can have time to study the lines one last time before setting the alarm for 4.30 a.m. and drifting off to sleep.

So it is a long day, but with a lot of hanging-about in between. With acting you cannot let the waiting get you down. Great discipline is required, so that after the hours of waiting you can still switch on the performance that is required in front of the camera. After all, the only thing that matters is what happens in front of the camera, that which is finally recorded for the finished film.

A friend of mine once described acting on film as 'being private in public'. An excellent description. With maybe a hundred pairs of eyes on you, you may have to pretend you are alone and cold in the middle of a swamp — whereas there are really hundreds of people standing just behind the camera, staring at you.

Rehearsals and takes

The sequence of filming is never the same as the sequence of the final film. The order of *shooting* is instead dictated by locations, so that all the scenes in one particular place are filmed at the same time, again for reasons of cost. This means that the actor must keep the line of the story clearly in his head, so that his behaviour in

The clapper/loader operating his clapperboard for Scene 166, Take 3. Note the sound boom and the chalk duster in his back pocket

the final edited sequence looks as if it is developing logically. Not easy to learn.

The sequence of each individual *set-up* for filming is as follows. The actors are called *on set* for a *line-up*. The director then *blocks* the scene. This also allows the *lighting cameraman* and all the other technicians to see clearly how the director intends the scene to be placed. After the line-up the actors go off to finish getting dressed and made-up, perhaps snatching a quick coffee or breakfast on the way. In place of the actors the *stand-ins* take over, doubling for the actors while the lights are placed and adjusted, cameras are moved into position, *props* are placed as required and whatever else may be needed is brought on.

About an hour later, when everything is in place, the actors are called back ('Can I have the first team please,' is the director's call) and actual rehearsals begin.

After detailed rehearsal, when the actors have made their contribution and the director has responded with final decisions, the scene is then ready to *shoot*.

The first assistant calls for total silence and checks that everyone is ready. Camera and sound are instructed to switch on ('turn over') and the clapper/loader (as in the photo) *marks* the scene for film and sound. Then when all is still and quiet the director calls out '*Action*' and the scene plays through. At the end he calls '*Cut*' and everything stops. If (as is usually the case) the scene needs to be repeated, everything is set up to go again and it becomes *Take two*. Each scene is usually *shot* several times, in several *takes*.

The sequence of filming within a scene is also intricate. First the *master shot* is completed, the key action in the scene, where all the actors are *in shot*. Then follow versions of the scene which may only include two or three actors out of the group. These are *two-shots* and *three-shots* where all the identical action of the original master shot is repeated but concentrated on only two or three actors at a time and at a closer distance. Finally the individual *close-ups* (also called *singles*) are shot to cement the detail of the scene. These can either be medium close-ups on a single actor reacting to the scene or a big close-up. Abbreviated these are known as MCU and BCU. A BCU is an actor's face writ VERY large on the screen indeed and used only for a very important reaction within a scene. When the director is satisfied that he has enough *in the can*, that scene is over and it is on to the next one.

Processing the film

Before leaving a scene the director finally instructs the *continuity clerk* as to which of the many takes he wants printed by the laboratories. He can already see which are likely to be the best versions.

When the *wrap* is called at the end of the day the precious cans of film are sent to the laboratory to be processed. Then if all is OK, *a clearance* is given by the lab. to the producer, who passes the approval back to the director.

On *Lionheart* the *film footage* was sent from Hungary to London by plane each night for

Preparing for a take

processing. The sound tapes went also so that sound could be matched to picture. Therefore the clearance by phone to the producer was essential in order to confirm that each day's filming was acceptable, with no technical faults.

A few days later that particular day's film with sound matched would arrive back for viewing. After work everyone could sit down for *the rushes*, to judge the quality of what they had done. The viewing usually happened every other night when another batch was flown in from London.

Cameras and sound

It is time now to talk of cameras and sound. The film company hires all the cameras and equipment from specialist hire firms, and the same is true for all the sound equipment. The camera team consists of the *lighting cameraman* (arguably the second, if not the first most important person on the set), the *camera operator*, *focus puller*, and *clapper/loader*. The person in charge of sound recording is the *sound recordist*, and his main aide is the *boom operator*. He is the one who holds the microphone, attached to a long pole, over the actors' heads (but always out of shot!). You need strong arms — I know, I tried it once.

Sometimes cameras are put up on top of a crane for a *wide shot*, to get a bird's eye view of the action below. The cranes are enormous but

A wide shot, from the top of a crane

highly manoeuvrable, and can swing up and down as required.

For close shots, the measuring tape you see in the picture on page 45 is used by the *focus-puller* to measure exactly how far the camera is from the actor: the closer the shot, the more critical and precise the focus has to be. When the camera is moving (*tracking* or *panning*) and the actors are also moving, the focus has to be constantly adjusted throughout the shot. Of course when the cameraman does a sudden *zoom* the focus-puller really must have his wits about him.

To cover a scene from different angles, the camera team would often shoot with two cameras running on the same scene, as in the picture on page 45 (top).

Once when a heavily-laden cart had to be sent tumbling down a steep incline, three cameras were used at once. They had to capture the

43

The camera operator (left) and focus-puller (right), back at ground-level

moment in one take as there was only one cart available and the evening light was failing fast. 'No mistakes permissible, PLEASE!' One of the three cameras was placed only feet from where the crashing cart, it was hoped, would finally come to rest. Luckily it all worked that time. But cameramen are often in the very front line of the 'battle', having to take precautions against real potential danger. It is the person in charge of *special effects* who takes these precautions, and plans the strategy in minute detail before even a foot of film is shot.

More cameras on location

45

Special effects

What do we mean by 'special effects'? Here is a definition from the retired head of photographic effects at the Walt Disney studio:

> A special effect is any technique or device that is used to create an illusion of reality in a situation where it is not possible, economical, or safe to use the real things.

And these special effects can be created in three different ways:

1. Using a whole range of models, miniatures, masks, stunt artists, etc. to pass for the actors, especially in long shots.
2. Cutting from one sequence of film to another, so that the eye does not notice the alternation between the real actor and the model.
3. Or combining images in 'composite photography', so that one character can be superimposed on a different background.

So our stunt artists in the battle scenes of *Lionheart* followed both of the first two principles of 'special effects'.

Lighting

The art of lighting in film work is highly creative: at its best it can be like an artist applying paint to a canvas — the *lighting cameraman* using filters and spots to colour and enhance whatever mood is required in a scene.

It is the Chief Electrician (known as the *gaffer*) who is responsible for putting all the required lighting equipment into the studio or location setting. It is called 'rigging the lights', and he is always helped by an assistant who is known as Best Boy. (I've yet to meet a Best Girl, but it cannot remain a male preserve for ever!)

With all the hardware of lighting set up, the lighting cameraman (known in the USA as Director of Photography) is then free to interpret the requirements of the director and create the mood required. The 'look' of a film is often a result of the harmony between the director and the lighting cameraman – translating the original vision of the film from the mind's eye into a screen image, or 'painting with light'.

Measuring the distance from the camera for the close-up shot. On the right is the chief electrician (*gaffer*) with his lamp on the left

47

Last minute work on costumes and props!

Building sets, making props

Another operation which is both time-consuming and labour-intensive is the building of sets and the assembling of *props*. The set designer, in this case a famous Spanish designer called Gil Parronda, was given a copy of the script many months before filming began. Much detailed discussion took place between Gil, the producers, Franklin (our director), Nana (our costume designer) and Josie, the *set dresser*, as to exactly what the overall style, the 'look' of the film would be. This was one reason why the costumes were not hired from stock or commissioned by one of the big firms: they wanted an overall design that had flair and was believably medieval. Gil, the producers, and Franklin then set off on a *recce* to both Hungary and Portugal to choose locations for all the scenes, and also to examine the facilities of the Hungarian studios that were to be used for all the *interiors*. Once chosen, and nearer the start of filming, both the *lighting cameraman* and the *camera operator* were shown the chosen locations so that they too could visualise in advance where each scene in the script would take place.

After all this research Gil sat down to design the necessary sets, and his drawings were then draughted into detailed plans for the construction of all the sets required. This took months.

Finally the work of building the sets began, with a huge team of plasterers, *chippies* and painters assembled from the UK, Portugal and Hungary. They needed enormous workshops and, despite endless mess along the way, they managed to produce wonderful sets, nearly all before filming began.

Because of the need for *weather cover* the sets had to be completed well in advance of when they might be needed. This meant that if the weather outside became too bad, the *shooting schedule* would be swiftly changed from the planned *exterior* scene to an alternative one inside the studio (an *interior*) so as not to lose shooting time. Of course if the weather outside had remained bad for too long all the sets available for interiors could even have been used up, and filming would have had to halt. Luckily that didn't happen with *Lionheart* but it did get very close. As a matter of fact on the four-month shoot the film ran only *two* days over the planned schedule. This is quite remarkable in film-making.

Working closely with Gil were the *property master*, Mickey, and his team. He and his main assistant, the *prop man*, were in charge of assembling all the objects and pieces of equipment necessary on the sets: chairs and tables, knives and spoons, all the food required in a scene, plus all the million and one other small details which suggest authentic surroundings. The *set dresser* was Gil Parronda's associate, Josie, whose job was to choose and design all the objects. Then it became the responsibility of Mickey and his team to find, often make, and finally place everything correctly on each set.

For instance, one scene even required a huge pie out of which would fly dozens of white doves. The sight of Mickey hidden out of sight of the camera beneath 'the pie', encouraging the doves to fly out when the pie was cut open, was amusing. On one take, only one dove peered out, causing everyone in the studio to *corpse*! (See the glossary for that word!) Then the task of catching them again (in between takes) was pretty difficult as you can imagine; some of the doves remained high up in the ceiling of the studio for days before they were finally caught!

The children

The unusual part about *Lionheart* was the large number of children needed for the crusade itself. Of these children the leading young actors (*principals*) were cast in the UK, with one notable exception: this was the young American actor who played my 'son' Robert, the 'star' of the movie, Eric Stolz. The other principal young actors were chosen from theatre schools in Britain, several of the older ones having just left drama school.

The crowds of other non-speaking children, of varying ages, were picked by Franklin in Hungary. A few of them came on with us to Portugal, as by then they were clearly *established* as recognisable faces in the film. Those in the

The Hungarian children setting out from 'Paris'

background of crowd scenes were necessarily left behind, and other children of similar appearance recruited in their place in Portugal.

You see here a group of very young Hungarian children in an action scene at 'the gates of Paris' (filmed in Budapest), as they set out on their crusade. The front and second rows are those who were lucky enough to be established and travelled on to Portugal with us.

It was very exiting for these children as they had never been outside their country before. They were looked after by official chaperones and teachers, as they were still quite young, and in spare moments the teachers were present to ensure that their education continued. Children are only allowed to work certain limited hours, and that regulation had to be strictly adhered to.

The cold and the delays were very tedious for

the younger children. So we all put in time at keeping them amused in either the breaks from filming or when they were not having lessons. We took turns to play games, football being a favourite. They were great fans of English football, although I have to admit that I, as a Rugby-Union-trained New Zealander, was not much of an advertisement for the game!

Many of the children were selected because of their specialised talents. Some were trained jugglers, and others excellent acrobats. Their adaptability and sense of fun contributed a lot to the liveliness of the scenes they were in.

But inevitably after a few weeks in Portugal some of the young Hungarian boys and girls started to get homesick. It is a tiring life for young children with too much energy to sit around and wait!

The jugglers and acrobats

The plot

The story of *Lionheart* was a scriptwriter's plot woven round the straight historical events, to make this film as memorable and enjoyable as the box office always requires. For a start there were two love stories in the film: one between my 'son' Robert and a poor country girl; the other between a young girl of noble birth who joined the crusade and a lowly but sprightly country lad. I won't tell you the outcome, as that would spoil your enjoyment of the film when it comes round. But I can tell you a bit more about the plot without giving too much away.

I was Simon Nerra, Duke of Brittany, a land-grabbing baron, always ready for a quick battle to win more territory. 'The House of Nerra will have gained enough land when the whole of France lies at its feet,' I snarl at someone.

Two of the peasant children together

Some of the children assembled

At the beginning of the story we are celebrating the fact that my son Robert will be knighted the next morning. Suddenly, into the midst of the revelry of the banquet in the Great Hall of my castle bursts Charles, my brother-in-law. He rides straight through the huge doorway mounted on his big steed, and gallops right up to my raised table. He is dressed in Crusader costume.

Before I have time to challenge him, he demands a release from his loyalty to me in order to ride off and join with Richard the Lionheart, on the great crusade. I refuse. As a result of this confrontation, in the big battle the next day my son Robert turns his magnificent white horse away from the bloodshed and rides off into the distance.

He arrives in Paris and there discovers a

separate quarter full of the city's poor. This is where he recruits his army of young children to start his own 'children's' crusade. The sets for these scenes were wonderful, suggesting a secret community hiding away in caves under the streets of Paris. It was known as the 'underground city'.

With many thrilling and dangerous adventures along the way, they all set off to meet up with their hero, Richard the Lionheart. They are pursued by the evil Black Prince, since every film needs its 'baddy' as well as its hero and love story.

The actual events of the Children's Crusade had a very unhappy end, and gave rise to several legends based on the story of the disappearing children. One of the best known is the Pied Piper of Hamelin.

The Black Prince, played by Gabriel Byrne

Portugal, a new location

After three months in Hungary the whole film unit moved to Portugal. Two big jets were used to carry all the technicians, actors and other staff and equipment. A lot more gear came by road, including some of the established horses; it was just like moving an army.

We flew south to a country that promised to be warm and sunny. We found the warmth but not the sun, at least not for the first two weeks. It poured with rain, day and night, but filming had to continue. We had no choice, as this time there was no weather cover. All the scenes required in Portugal were exteriors.

Large umbrellas had to cover the cameras and equipment, and the crew were wrapped up in waterproof clothing. But the actors, out in front of the cameras in the full force of the deluge, looked (and were) very wet indeed. It was a nightmare for the wardrobe department, as costumes became drenched; and for the make-up department as well, as make-up became smudged; and not least for Meinir and her assistants as neat wigs and hair became soaked.

Eventually the skies cleared, and we were able to enjoy the sun and the sea, and in our spare time visit the wonderful sea-food restaurants, to eat really fresh fish, perfectly cooked.

We filmed on beaches, on cliffs and up in the lush green hills. One location was a two-hour drive from our hotel so we had four hours'

The actress Deborah Leigh Moore, after we'd travelled to Portugal

travelling that day. While I was waiting between takes, I took my horse at a full gallop along the most beautiful white sandy beach imaginable, with an exhilarating wind behind me. By the time I had got to the far end of the beach they needed me on set, and had to use a megaphone to call me back!

Our filming ended with another big battle on the Portuguese location...more 'blood', more soldiers crashing off horses and footsoldiers 'stabbing' and in turn being 'stabbed.' All the same meticulous rehearsal was necessary again.

My final appearance came at the end of the film, as father and son are touchingly reunited. There will not be a dry eye in the house when you see that ending, I hope.

The end?

Suddenly it was our last day. Time to say our goodbyes and go our separate ways. The *wrap party* went on late into the night, with even the youngest of the child actors allowed to join in and celebrate the months we had shared. Friendships had developed, and yet now we were to be divided by distance between our various towns, cities and countries, knowing we would never again come together in exactly that combination of people. We danced and swapped jokes as the party, half a celebration and half a 'wake', went on into the early hours.

The next day meant packing, then off to the airport. All farewells were made, with promises to keep in touch, at least by letter.

The camaraderie of being part of a film unit, away from home in another country, is hard to imagine if you have never had that experience. It had been a great time but now it was over for most of us. For others, though, it was just the start of another crucial process in film-making.

Two stuntmen rehearse a sword-fight on horseback, during our last days in Portugal

Editing, post-synching

In the months that followed, Franklin and his editor got down to the work of editing the film, cutting it into its final shape. All the many separate shots we had taken were put into sequence, sound effects were added and the whole pace of the film was created. The final editing took place in Los Angeles. Then the composer was called in to see the film and set about composing suitable music, orchestrating it and then recording for Franklin and his editor to add to the almost completed film.

One other final stage is called *post-synching*. Months after filming is completed the principal actors, myself included, are called back to the studio. Franklin came to London and we met in a recording room at Twickenham Studios. It was a happy reunion, and an interesting chance to see scenes from the film up on the screen.

The process of *post-synching*, or *dubbing* or *looping* (all three terms are used but mean the same thing), means re-recording some of the lines to get the quality of the sound more perfect than could be achieved on location. I therefore had to say the lines over again, matching the movement of my own lips precisely to my image on the screen (known as *lip-synching*).

It was a strange experience coming back five months after filming. There was *Lionheart* projected in nearly finished form and I had to slot myself back into the spirit of my performance, months after the event. This time it took only three quarters of an hour to re-record my lines, in straight sequence.

It had been an eventful five months since completion of the filming. Between the wrap on *Lionheart* and the post-synching I'd worked on two more films and a TV play. By chance I met up again with Gil (the designer) and Raphael (the caterer) on one of the two films which was made in Spain, their home territory. After the post-synching we all exchanged news and then parted again. The next time we would meet would be at the premiere.

Publicity

The other important job to be done at this stage is publicity.

The man in charge of publicity was a charming American called Hunt Downs, who worked with a very capable Hungarian assistant, Christine. Hunt and Christine often joined us on location in both Hungary and Portugal. They brought a *stills photographer* to take lots of pictures of the action for use in later publicity. You cannot just extract stills from the filming; they have to be specially-taken individual shots.

The objective of Hunt's department, up until the day of the launch of the film, is to muster maximum publicity in magazines, newspapers, radio and television. During that period I saw a piece in a London newspaper about one of our leading actresses, Deborah Leigh Moore, pictured at Heathrow Airport with her father Roger Moore, of James Bond fame. *Lionheart* got its mention: all good advance notice for the film.

As the film premiere draws closer the volume of publicity grows, with the design of posters and handbills, ads and previews, and personal appearances by the stars on TV and in magazine interviews, etc. What the publicity people have to create is a continuous visual reminder that the public will associate with the title, and big names, to entice them to the box-office.

Finis

The film itself builds up to the grand climax of the premiere, as if it had a life and momentum of its own. For the actors, though, there is more often the anti-climax of returning home. The only relief is the arrival of the paycheque for all the hours of work on the film. That is some compensation, but then you start waiting once more, in the hope of the next job turning up.

So here I am again at the top of a step-ladder, the old familiar story: paint-pot balanced, brush poised, out of work and filling in time with some home-decorating whilst waiting for that phone to ring...hold on...is it?...yes, it *is* ringing. Mind the paint pot!

INTERIOR: PAINT POT AND BRUSH PUT DOWN CAREFULLY. THE ACTOR RUNS TO THE TELEPHONE, TRIPPING OVER THE SLEEPING DOG ON HIS WAY. HE LIFTS THE RECEIVER. PAINT ALL OVER THE HANDSET. DOG BARKS.

ACTOR: (TO DOG)
Be quiet! (INTO THE PHONE) Hello.
HE LISTENS TO THE VOICE ON THE LINE.
Yes...yes...yes, I would be *very* interested.
PAUSE AS HE LISTENS AGAIN.
Did you say Timbuktu? Yes, I'd love to take it.
THE END
ROLL CREDITS

The unit list

The 'unit list' is issued to every participant who joins the group. Just add up how many people are involved behind the camera!

Two Executive Producers
Two Producers
The Director
The Editor and his assistants
Production Supervisor
Two Production Managers
Production Assistant and Assistant to Producer
London Contact at Pinewood Studios
First, Second and Third Assistant Directors
Continuity Clerk
Unit Driver, in London
Chaperone for the English children and many others for the Hungarian and Portuguese children, plus teachers. Several Portuguese and Hungarian liaison and public relations people
Production Accountant, Assistant Accountant and Cashier plus other accounting staff for the Portuguese and Hungarians
Production Designer
Art Director
Two Design Draughtsmen, plus many plasterers, painters and carpenters
Set Decorator
Property Buyer
Lighting Cameraman
Camera Operator
Focus-puller
Clapper/Loader
Grip

Titan Crane Operator
Sound Recordist
Boom Operator
Casting Directors (USA and UK)
Construction Manager and Assistant, plus
  local staff
Chief Make-up and Assistant
Hair Department both Chief and Assistant,
  plus many others for local Hungarian and
  Portuguese extras
Property Master and Prop Man plus local help
Costume Designer
Wardrobe Mistress and three assistants plus
  many local staff and numbers of Dressers.
Chief Electrician (Gaffer)
Best Boy/Generator Driver
Hungarian and Portuguese assistants to Gaffer
Five Caterers, plus many local staff
Director of Publicity with an assistant and
  secretary
Stills Photographer
Special Effects Supervisor, Assistants and staff
Stunt Co-ordinator, Horsemaster and two main
  grooms plus dozens of Hungarian grooms
  and Portuguese Army soldiers
Twenty-five Actors (Principals)
Several hundred Extras, dozens of children,
  many stunt people, lots of riders, stand-ins
  to double for actors
Transport Managers and assistants
Twenty-five drivers in each country
Several interpreters in both countries
Both Hungarian and Portuguese First, Second
  and Third Assistant Directors
The many workers in Italy, Hungary and
  Portugal who helped make the costumes
The Falconer!

Glossary

'Action' — The command from the director to commence filming a scene.

Blocks — Working out the actors' moves in a scene is known as blocking.

Call sheet — The printed pages of instructions for the following day's filming, telling all involved exactly which scenes will be shot and when and where to turn up.

Camera operator — The person who looks through the viewfinder and operates the camera.

Cast — To 'be cast' is to be chosen for an acting job, and 'the cast' is the list of actors involved.

Chippies — Carpenters.

Clapper/Loader — Member of the camera crew in charge of loading and unloading film from the camera. He also 'marks' with the clapper-board the beginning and end of each take, chalking up the scene and take-numbers on the board. The sound made by the clapper-board is to help check that the sound (dialogue, etc.) is matched to picture.

Clearance — Being told you can go home or have finished your work entirely on a film. You also need assurance from the lab. that the development of the film is technically acceptable.

Close-up — A very close shot of an actor. BCU and MCU are abbreviations for Big Close-up and Medium Close-up.

Continuity — The person in charge of ensuring continuity of detail between one take and the next. For instance, one cannot have an actor disappear through a door with a hat on and appear on the other side with no hat and wearing different trousers!

Contract	The agreement between actor and film company, specifying money and all terms.
Corpse	When one laughs uncontrollably at a funny situation.
Crowd extras	All the people in the background of a shot, who generally have no lines to say.
'Cut'	The instruction given by the director at the end of each take for filming to stop.
Cutting room	The place where the editing is done.
Director	The person in charge of directing the action of the film and later editing it. He 'creates' the film and is in total control of every aspect of the filming.
Dressers	The people in charge of helping actors on and off with their costumes, and checking the detail of the individual actor's costume.
Dubbing	Re-recording dialogue in a sound studio after the film has completed shooting, to improve the quality of the sound. Also called looping and post-synching.
Editing room	Where the picture is cut together into its final sequence. Also referred to as the cutting room.
Established	When something or someone has been seen, and therefore remembered, in a shot.
Exterior	A scene that takes place outside.
Extras	The non-speaking parts who act as crowd, villagers, soldiers, riders, etc.
Film footage	The film that's been shot and is safely 'in the can'.
Film unit	All the people involved in the making of a film.
First assistant	The director's right-hand person. A very important job on a film. In charge of getting everyone and everything in place as swiftly as possible on set. A good first assistant is invaluable.

First team	The director's reference to the principal actors coming back on set to replace the stand-ins and start rehearsal. Not a common term but certainly one used by Franklin Schaffner. An American term.
Focus-puller	The member of the camera staff who sits to the side of the camera and adjusts the focus as and when required by the camera operator. During a shot the focus may change constantly.
Freeze-frame	Stopping the action of a film by freezing the image.
Gaffer	Chief electrician on a film, in overall charge of lights.
Interior	Scene filmed inside a studio set or inside a building.
In the can	The film is placed literally in a strong canister after shooting, on its way to and from the lab. So when a scene is 'in the can' it has actually been shot.
Lighting cameraman	The person who controls the light of every scene of a film. This person is in charge of the cameras and when scenes are being shot outdoors, has to respond to variations in light by instructing the chief electrician (gaffer) where to put lamps, then tell the camera operator what adjustments are needed in the camera itself. A very important job, and it is always essential to get the best lighting cameraman available when making a film. In shipboard terms he's the director's chief engineer.
Line-up	The placement of actors and technicians on a new set, so that everyone can see what problems will need to be solved in that scene.
Location	The place where filming is taking place when not in a film studio.
Marks	The chalk-marks on the clapper-board, indicating which scene it is and what take-number. Essential for the later editing of scenes.

Master shot	A shot of the entire scene with everything and everyone visible in the scene. This is always shot first.
Night shoot	Filming at night, invariably an exterior. A lot of low-budget films shoot 'day for night' using a special filter on the lens, so their night scene can actually be shot during the day.
Panning	The movement of the camera swinging to the left or right, sometimes to shoot the full breadth of a scene, sometimes a more limited movement.
Post-synching	Synchronisation of voice to lips on the completed film, done in a recording studio long after the shooting has finished and the film has been edited. Also referred to as looping or dubbing.
Principal actors	The main actors who have lines to speak.
Producer	The person or persons in overall charge of the finance, control and planning of a film. An executive producer is the one in total control but often based back at head office whereas the 'line' producer is the person on the spot who controls day-to-day planning of finance and schedules.
Property master	The person in overall charge of the supply or making of all bits and pieces (props) required on a set. He is usually not on-set himself, but his on-the-spot representative is the prop man.
Props	See under 'Property master'
Recce (pronounced Rekky)	An abbreviation of reconnaissance. Before filming starts, the director travels around to view likely locations for each scene. Specialist firms can be hired to make suitable suggestions.
'Rolling'	The film has been switched on in the camera just prior to filming a scene.

'Running'	Sound-recording machine has been switched on ready to hear the dialogue and other sound in a scene.
Running buffet	The food is laid out and you eat when you have time to spare, there being no 'official' break for refreshment. This is quite common when a film is getting seriously behind schedule.
Rushes	The film to be viewed when it returns from the lab. Americans call it 'the dailies' as they usually come back from the lab. each day and are viewed in the evening after the day's shooting is over.
Second assistant	The second most important assistant director, who obeys the instructions of the first assistant. In charge of the printing out of the call-sheets, getting people from *a* to *b*, etc.
Set	The room or building built to film any one particular scene, or the area used for a scene outside.
Set designer	Designs all sets required.
Set dresser	The person in charge of choosing or designing the objects required on a set. The property master and property buyer work closely in collaboration.
Set-up	Literally means set up to do a scene in a film or part of a scene.
Shooting	Filming.
Shooting schedule	The plan for when each scene will be filmed. A lot of pre-filming advance work is done, but often changes occur daily in the schedule if bad weather, accidents, or sudden unavailability of locations occur, for whatever reason.
Shooting script	The script that is the final version used for the filming.

Shot	One piece of film, e.g. 'We got a marvellous shot of the cart going over the cliff.'
Single	Another word for close-up (which is explained earlier in this Glossary).
Special effects (SFX)	Get it? Special Eff-ects (FX). The people in charge of a lot of difficult effects like explosions, small models that look like the real thing, fog, mist, you name it, they can do it. Very expert and imaginative, and can make anything work.
Staged	When the action is placed on a particular set ready to be filmed.
Stand-in	Someone employed to stand in place of the actor while lights are adjusted, prior to shooting a scene. Also known as a double.
Studio	A specially-built, sound-proofed building where interior scenes are shot. Also known as a Sound Stage.
Take	A scene being filmed: 'Take One', 'Take Two', etc.
Third assistant	Answerable to the second assistant. Often the general 'dogsbody' of the hierarchy of assistant directors. Gets good training in the ins and outs of film-making. Spends a lot of time running on behalf of others, and is sometimes referred to as 'a runner'.
Three-shot	A shot of only three actors in a scene.
Tracking	When rails are put down to move the camera forwards or backwards.
'Turn over'	Instructions by the director for sound and camera to switch on prior to filming a scene.
Two-shot	A shot of only two actors in a scene.
Unit	The whole film crew.

Weather cover	The set built inside a studio (sound-stage) to be used if the weather outside is bad and the planned schedule has to change from an exterior scene to an interior one.
Wide shot	When the camera is distant from the action, taking in a wide area.
Wrap	When filming finishes at the end of the day, or when filming finishes entirely at the completion of the film.
Wrap-party	The party held at the end to celebrate the finish of filming on a picture. In the theatre it would be called the 'last-night' party.
Zoom	When the camera lens alters rapidly from a distant shot right in to a close shot. Or a zoom can be from a close shot to a wider shot of the action, and this is often done more slowly than the 'zoom-in'.

Book list

Some books on the subject of film-making and TV work which you might enjoy reading are:

Susan Meredith and Phil Mottram, *Films and Special Effects* (Usborne)
Chris Moore, *Film Studio* (Behind the Scenes series, Franklin Watts)
The English Centre, *Narrative and Film*
Ed Naha, *The Making of 'Dune'* (W.H. Allen/Target)
Mike Beynon, *Making a TV Programme* (R & D series, Macmillan Education)